The Complete Technique and Syllabus for Tango Milonga
Intermediate
by
Andre Beaulne

The official manual for the
Canadian Dancesport Federation

2020
Timewrite publishing company limited

Important Notice
No part of this book may be reproduced in any form or by any electronic or mechanical means (including information storage and retrieval systems) without written permission from the author/publisher, Andre Beaulne.

Published by Timewrite Publishing
Copyright © 2020 Andre Beaulne Inc.
All rights reserved, including the right of reproduction in whole or in part, in any form.

Design and layout by Andre Beaulne

Also by Andre Beaulne:

The Complete Technique and Syllabus for Tango Milonga
Beginner
January 2020

by
Andre Beaulne

The Complete Technique and Syllabus for Tango Milonga

15 Step Variations for Intermediate Dancers

Tango Milonga

by Andre Beaulne

Intermediate

A technique manual for CDF's Argentine Tango Milonga syllabus figures. Canadian Dancesport Federation

Table of Contents

Thank You	Page 6
Author's Note	Page 7
About the Author	Page 8
Trio of the Argentine Tango	Page 9
Milonga & Music	Page 10
Dance Tips	Page 15
The Basic 8	Page 18
Reading the Charts	Page 20
Tango Milonga Step List	Page 23
Charts	Page 24
Canadian Dance Federation (CDF) Programs	Page 54

Thank You!

Acknowledgements

Putting together this book was a vast undertaking and I would like to sincerely thank all of those directly and indirectly involved.

First and foremost I would like to thank my wife, Francine. She is my sounding board, my editor, and basically, my everything.

Thank you to Paul Varro who kindly wrote about the music and math of the Tango Milonga.

Thank you to the Canadian Dancesport Federation (CDF) Board of Directors for approving this Intermediate Milonga Manual.

With regards to the book production, my sincere gratitude to Claire & Rheal Perron for their expert assistance.

Author's Note

Argentine Tango is a social dance based on improvisation, although there are fixed patterns sometimes used in lessons. The dance is alive and spontaneous. I hope this manual will complement your Tango Salon as well as Tango Vals. Many steps can be danced to all three styles, however, Milonga tends to be kept to more simple moves.

With time you should be able to include the patterns presented using the awareness of your partner and the music to dance fluidly in an improvised manner. Tango has technique, musicality, and improvisation.

This manual can be a perfect tool. Easy-to-follow dance steps enable you to study the steps at home in your own pace.

Andre Beaulne
Head of Argentine Tango Department
Canadian Dancesport Federation (CDF)
National Argentine Tango Examiner for CDF

Andre Beaulne
Head of National Argentine Tango Department for CDF
Fellow Argentine Tango CDF
National Argentine Tango Examiner for CDF
Fellow International Standard CDF
Fellow International Latin CDF
Professional Judge, Dance Choreographer/Performer

Most of Andre's Argentine Tango training was completed in Buenos Aires. He has been trained by Argentine Tango legends: Jorge Torres, Juan Carlos Copes, Jorge Firpo, Gustavo Naviera, Giselle Anne, Rosalia Gasso, Alejandro Barrientos, Gustavo Rosas, Gisela Natoli, Esteban Cortez, Evelyn Rivera, Christy Cote and more...

Andre also teaches Ballroom Dancing, at all levels from Beginner to Championship. He teaches many styles including: Social American Style, International Style, Salsa, West Coast Swing and more. Most of his Ballroom/Latin training was with Claire Perron, Pierre Allaire, Mireille Veilleux, Pierrette Chartier, France Mousseau and Jean-Marc Généreux.

www.francineandre.com

Ottawa, Canada

Dance Art by Andre
www.artbyandre.ca

Trio of the Argentine
Tango Salon - Tango Vals - Tango Milonga

Argentine Tango is rich with tradition and history.

Tango is a dance and music that originated in Buenos Aires at the turn of the century, developing in the melting pot of cultures that was Buenos Aires. Immigrants from Europe mixed with earlier generations of settlers of all races and from South American countries and brought their native music and dances with them. Traditional Polkas, Waltzes, and other dances were mixed in with the popular Habanera from Cuba to form a new dance and music, the Milonga.

There are three types of Tango dances, each with its own character and music.

Tango Salon -
Salon Tango is danced socially in Buenos Aires and around the world. It is the most common style of Tango. Salon Tango was danced throughout the Golden Era of Argentine Tango. (1935–1952) Full Tango orchestras performed and Tango was danced in large venues. Salon Tango is often characterized by slow measured, and smoothly executed moves. The couple embraces closely, having a flexible embrace, opening slightly to make room for various figures and closing again. Argentine Tango is danced counterclockwise around the outside of the dance floor respecting the space of other dancers on the floor.

Note:
Show Tango is a more theatrical form of Argentine Tango. This might be the most often seen by the public, which is breathtaking. Show Tango routines includes embellishments, acrobatics, and solo moves that would be impractical on a social dance floor.

Tango Vals -
Musical phrases of Vals are fast-paced, inviting the dancers to move from one movement to the next as if "on the go". Tango Vals music is based on the classic 1-2-3 of Waltz, but in this type of Tango, dancers typically dance on the one (the first beat). The music is played in ¾ time at a slow, medium or fast tempo. Tango Vals is danced in a rather relaxed, smooth flowing dancing style in contrast to Viennese Waltz where often 3 steps per measure are taken and turn almost constantly. Experienced dancers alternate the smooth one-beat-per-measure walk with some double-time steps, stepping on one, two or all three beats in a measure. Tango Vals dancing is characterized by an absence of pauses and instead features continual turns in both directions.

Tango Milonga -
Milonga paved the way for Tango and it was from Milonga that steps were taken and adapted to the Salon style. Many patterns are common to both dances. Milonga is the oldest form of Tango with a strong emphasis on having a multitude of various built in rhythms.

In the 1920's orchestras started to play tangos slower and in 4/4 timing with smooth and even time between beats, but before this time, all Tangos were played as Milongas with syncopated rhythms. Even the most famous song "La Cumparsita" was originally written with a syncopated 2/4 Milonga rhythm.

Milonga is 2/4 timing. Meaning that there are 2 beats per measure. Salon Tango music is 4/4 timing, meaning that there are 4 beats per measure. Step on the 1st and 3rd beat of a Tango, and the 1st beat of Milonga.

The word 'Milonga' has 3 definitions.
1.) It refers to the dance party.
2.) It refers to a musical style of music.
3.) It refers to the dance itself.

The Milonga originated as a form of song and from these folk-singers the dance became a variation from this music. With a simplified music tempo, dancers acquired new and simple steps. Milonga evolved based on a mix of steps from a variety of other dances. It was inspired from the steps of African slaves in Argentina, from the Cubans in Buenos-Aires, and the Polka of Czechoslovakia, then became known as a Milonga.

Movement is normally faster than that of the Tango Salon or Tango Vals, and pauses are less common. It is usually danced without complicated figures, with a more humorous and rustic style in contrast with the often serious and dramatic Tango.

Music: There are different styles of Milonga:

Milonga music was derived from the songs of the exciting Cuban habanera. The song was set to a lively tempo, as are most Milongas.

Habanera Rhythm: a Cuban rhythm that started back in the 1830's.
The rhythm, referred to as a "Habanera" rhythm is what gives Milonga a distinctly different dance style and a much greater depth of improvisation. When Milonga is danced including both single and syncopated rhythms, it gives the dancer an incredible array of rhythms, instruments, melodies, and vocals in which to work with, helping to create a truly improvised and unique dance!

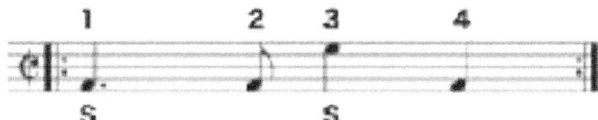

♩.	1½ beats	A dotted quarter note lasts for one and a half beats.
♪	½ beat	An eighth note, also called a quaver, is played for one eighth the duration of a whole note
♩	1 beat	A quarter note is one-fourth the time value of a whole note.

To dance "habanera rhythm", step on all 4 counts: on 1, then 2-3 and on 4. Note that there is a 1/8 note on the 2 count. You can think of it as: 1, &3,4 count or S, &QQ count. See the music chart above and notice how close together the 2 and 3 counts are. If you dance the habanera rhythm you match the music.

In this technique manual, we will use the following rhythms:

To dance "milonga lisa", meaning smooth, These steps are generally on every slow count. (down-beat) Two numbers represent one slow.

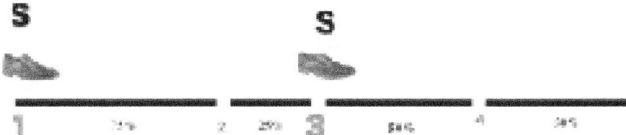

To dance "milonga traspié", add syncopations, steps using double beat on a quick-quick count. (2 steps in 1 Beat) Traspié means "trip". Dancers play with the beat to syncopate the Tango steps.

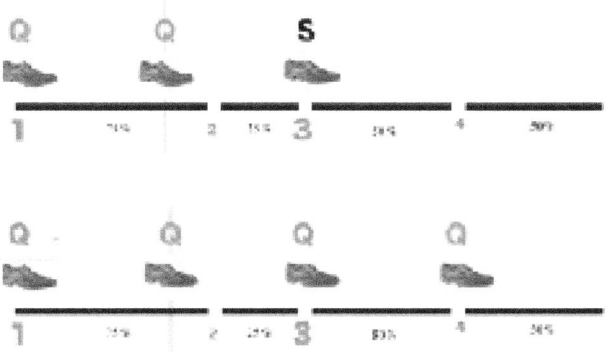

Other rhythms :
Pausing rhythms (1/2 time) where we dance only on the 1 out of 4 beats.
Corrida rhythms where we dance on all 4 of 4 beats (double time).
Dancers sometimes use double or triple time over two beats.
Double on one beat and Triple on two beats.

The genre of Milonga music originated in the region of Río de la Plata in Argentina and Uruguay. The popular Tango music was first danced in the neighbourhoods of Buenos Aires and Montevideo. Milonga is a style of music that reached the height of its popularity around the 1870s. It is a segment of rhythmic drumming.
There are many rhythms to choose from when dancing the Milonga. A Musician understands there are many rhythms within the downbeats.

Milonga Rhythms 4/4 Timing	1	2	3	4
Pausing	S			
Walking	S		S	
QQS	Q	Q	S	
SQQ	S		Q	Q
Corrida	Q	Q	Q	Q

The Math - The Structure of Tango

Classic Tango songs are typically constructed around a predictable mathematical formula consisting of: 3 different melodies, let's call them A, B, C.
There are 5 parts in total, typically occurring A, B, A, C, A

This general structure is not guaranteed. Sections A, B, A, C, A can be longer or shorter or have intros to the sections. It is only a guide to listen for. Listen to hear when these sections are coming to an end and when a new one begins.

Each segment has exactly 64 Orchestra beats for a total of 320 orchestra beats per song. There are 4 phrases in each part with a minor cadence 1/2 way through each part (beat 32) ending in a major cadence at the end of each 64 beat melody. Try not to dance through a cadence as it looks like you are rushing and not respecting the pause in the music. It would be like talking without using commas or periods in a conversation, ignoring punctuation.

Classic Tango is 4/4 timing with 4 beats per bar. The notation 4/4 means 4 quarter notes to a bar of music, so 4 X 1/4 = 1 bar. There are even and equal amounts of time between musical beats.

Music is written in bars, so there are 80 bars of music in each song typically. There might be a lead in or introduction, but we don't count that in the body of the song.

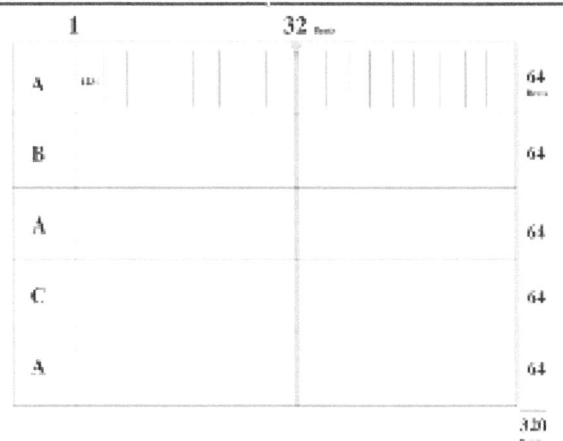

1 Song = 5 Parts
1 Measure = 4 Beats (Bar of music)
1 Phrase = 4 Measures = 16 Beats
1 Part = 4 Phrases = 64 Beats

Total = 320 Beats

The song will end with a final musical cadence at beat # 320 where dancers should try to stop moving on time to match the finality of the orchestra. At the end of a song, there is a falling down of the melody like a period at the end of a sentence. Adjust your figure or movement to stop precisely when the orchestra stops. Looks great!

The 6 Count Basic - the Baldosa Box

The basic movement or root figure in Milonga does not include a ladies cross that was introduced in the late 1900's, but is rather based upon a box (more like a rectangle) called a "Baldosa". Translated from Spanish this means a floor tile and is also the name of a famous Milonga (place of dance) in Buenos Aires.

Milonga was invented somewhere between 40 and 60 years before the invention of the ladies cross in Tango. The Baldosa box in its simplest form; side, forward, forward, side, back, back, is non-traveling basic that only requires 6 beats to complete. From this basic box derive all the possible basic steps in the Tango family; each free foot can only go forward, side, or back. Step repetitions, weight changes in place, interruptions/reversals, and pivots are all added to this 6 count basic to make up an endless variety of figures.

Generally speaking, it is noted that dancers should do weight changes at least 4 times in a bar of music as Milonga does not have the dramatic movements of Tango that invite long pauses and holding position. So "step on every beat" (counting in 4's) is a good guideline of Milonga and "step on more than every beat" makes the dance even more interesting.

The 1 beat in each bar is the most important and is rarely missed. Start on a 1, end on a 1.

Good examples of music to dance the Milonga:
Milonga sentimental - Orquesta tipica Francisco Canaro
Milonga De Mis Amores - Francisco Canaro.

Dance Tips

Note that if you use a back start, **don't dance directly back into other dancers behind you**. In a particularly crowded dance floor, omit the back start completely.

Things to Think About

First:
Find the Beat!
Most beginner dancer's start by stepping on the "compas", or the strong beat. The place in the music where it feels natural to clap is where you step.
Next:
Recognize that the music comes in "phrases", and usually in intervals of 8 strong beats, 4 bars, 7 steps then a pause. (But not always the case)
Next:
Recognize that there are different orchestras. Each has its own way of playing or interpreting tango music. These differences can be used in your dancing.
Next:
Connect "feeling" with "dancing". Express how you feel with the music.
Next:
Find a connection with your partner. Paying attention to the person you are dancing with has to be happening all the time. This mutual awareness is the best source of creativity.

Amount of Turn

The amount of turn is measured between the feet. When the follower is circling around the leader, sometimes it is best to just follow the shoulders and not think about the foot positions or amount of turn.

Note: While dancing turning steps such as the Molinete, the rotation is alway fluid in one direction with the body moving evenly throughout even if the feet are moving and pointing different directions.

Milonga is not simply dancing Tango Salon faster. It has its own unique style. Use small and simple steps. The steps are much smaller than the Tango Vals and Tango Salon. The Embrace is closer allowing for constant connection. Tango is danced by two people for each other.

The quick movements do not allow for complicated movements or sequences so keep it simple.
Dance without transferring your full weight. Keep the centre of your body weight between both feet. Express playfully.

Choose places in the music to pause or to go quicker. The character of the Milonga is in the variations of tempo.

Parallel System or Cross System.

Tango is danced in either Parallel System or Cross System. The leader can change his weight from one foot to another while the follower's weight remains unchanged; this is the simplest method of changing from a parallel system to a cross-system or vice versa.
Walking in the parallel system: leader and follower are stepping with legs opposite each other (mirroring each other's steps)
Walking in the cross-system: Leaders and followers are using the same foot at each step. (leader and follower use the right foot at the same time, or left foot at the same time)

Closed Hold: The dancers' chests are closer to their partner than their hips, and often there is contact at about the level of the chest (the contact point differing, depending on the height of the leader and the closeness of the embrace). The leader and the follower's chests are in contact and they are dancing with their heads touching or very near each other. The embrace is face to face danced in a close embrace. The leader's right arm extends as far as possible, without squeezing, around the follower's back.

Footwork: How to step forward is a feeling and choice you will have to make as a dancer. I would get different answers from various Tango masters. While some lead with a toe, others prefer to lead with a heel. I vary how I step while considering many elements: how my partner is moving, the music and how I want to represent my movement at that particular time. The size of step decides if I dance with a heel or toe lead. Make the step as natural as possible, without overthinking it.

Building Figures
Steps are joined together to build complete figures, much like a puzzle. These groups can be repeated or followed by any other groups in this manual. As you learn and progress you will find that elements of any group can be mixed with any other group. The most important aspect of dancing is to enjoy what you are doing.

The Salida
The opening movement is called the Salida. However, the Salida incorporates many varied starting elements. The Reverse or Back Start is the most easily lead but must be considered very carefully, especially, on a crowed dance floor. In this manual I have included many different opening movements so the leader can make good decisions on where to safely dance on the dance floor.

The Resolution
The Tango Close is a 3-step closing finish. In this movement, please allow the step to resolve gently. It is the most common ending of a figure and leaves the dancers on the appropriate foot, ready to start the next step.

Disassociation
Refers to the top half of the body rotating to the left or to the right, as one unit, around the spinal column of the dancer, independently of the lower half of the body.

Basic 8 Step
I have included a chart of the Basic 8 from the Tango Salon.
We will refer to this figure for the dance positions.
On a crowded dance floor please eliminate step #1 and begin with step #2.

The basic figure is used for education purposes. The dancer always improvises so you might never dance the complete pattern of the basic step of Tango. The basic 8 steps are composed of back step, side step, cross for the follower, forward step, and sidestep. Basic steps can also be divided into four phases:
Salida - A beginning or start of your dancing: (position 1 and 2)
Caminada - the walks (position 3 and 4)
Cross - (position 5)
Resolution - (positions 6,7,8)

Parallel System Basic
Leader

Commence FDW

Step#	Foot Position	Count	Turn (Feet)	Summary	Beat
1	RF Back	S	Nil	Salida Back	1,2
2	LF Side	S	1/8 Left (Body Turns Less)		3,4
3	RF Forward *(CBMP) OP	S	Nil	Caminada	5,6
4	LF Forward LSL	S	Nil		7,8
5	RF Closes to LF	S	Nil	Follower's Cross	1,2
6	LF Forward	S	Nil	Resolution	3,4
7	RF Side	S	Nil		5,6
8	LF Closes to RF	S	Nil		7,8

Note: Please take a very small step back on step #1 and avoid dancing against the LOD. Do not dance backing into other dancers behind you.

* Contrary Body Movement Position *(CBMP) - This is the action of placing one leg forward & across or behind & across the body without the body turning. It is, therefore, a foot position. CBMP is used on all outside steps to prevent loss of contact from the embrace. If the leader merely stepped straight forward, contact would be lost.*

Parallel System Basic
Follower

Commence BDW

Step#	Foot Position	Count	Turn (Feet)	Summary	Beat
1	LF Forward	S	Nil	Salida	1,2
2	RF Side	S	1/8 Left (Body Turns Less)		3,4
3	LF Back (CBMP)	S	Nil	Caminada	5,6
4	RF Back RSL	S	Nil		7,8
5	LF Crosses in Front of RF (Cruzada)	S	Nil	Follower's Cross	1,2
6	RF Back	S	Nil	Resolution	3,4
7	LF Side	S	Nil		5,6
8	RF Closes to LF	S	Nil		7,8

Note: On step #4, take a long step back to allow an easy cross. On step #5 (the cross) try to be in front of the leader.

Direction of Steps
1. Down the LOD
2. Against the LOD
3. To Centre
4. To Wall
5. Diagonal to Centre
6. Diagonal to Centre Against LOD
7. Diagonal to Wall
8. Diagonal to Wall Against LOD

Position of the Body in the Room
1. Facing LOD
2. Backing LOD
3. Facing Centre
4. Facing Wall
5. Facing Diagonal Centre
6. Backing Diagonal Wall Against LOD
7. Facing Diagonal Wall
8. Backing Diagonal Wall Against LOD

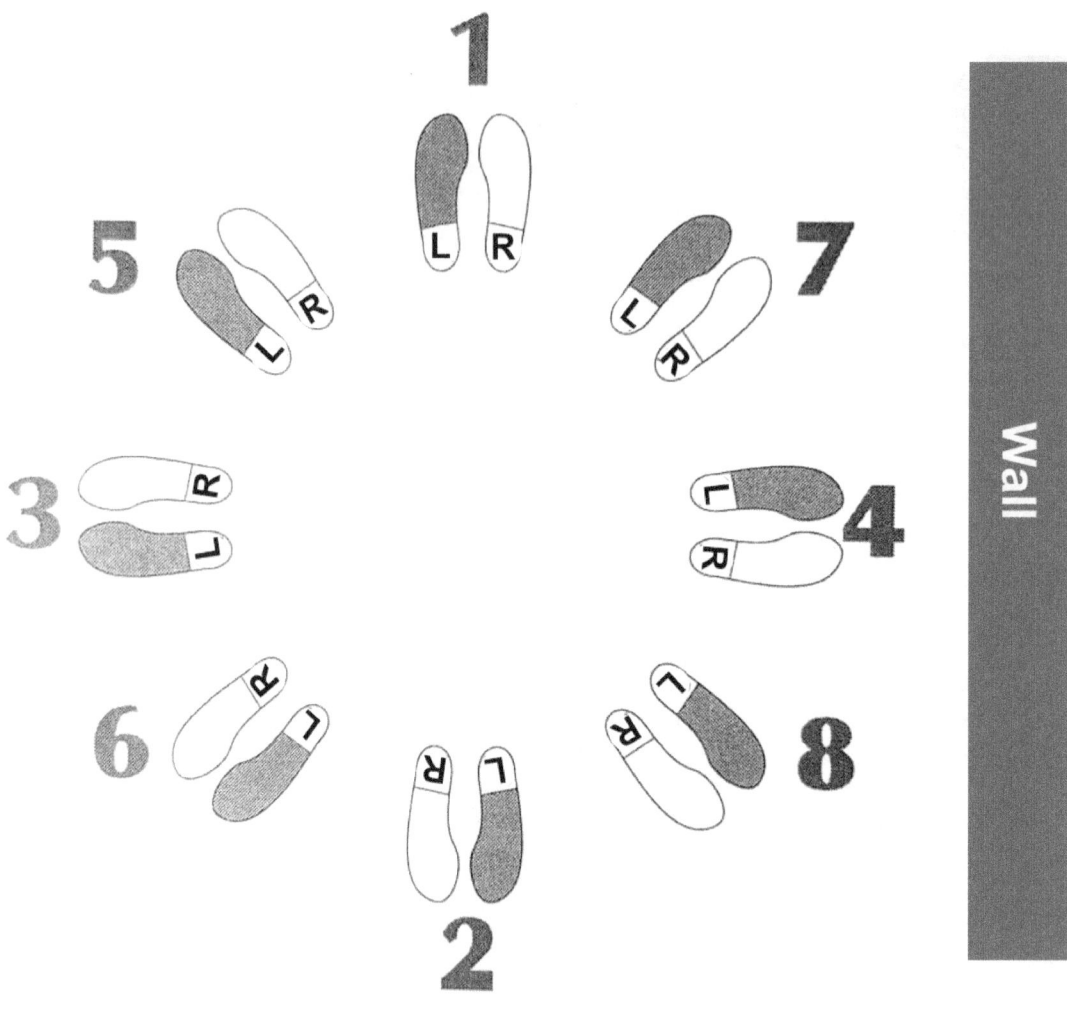

Dance Chart courtesy of Claire Perron.

Direction of Dancing

How does one orient oneself on the dance floor? All movement is in a counter clockwise direction; therefore from any position on the floor, face the closest wall, always travel left. That direction is shown below by an imaginary line called the line of dance (LOD).

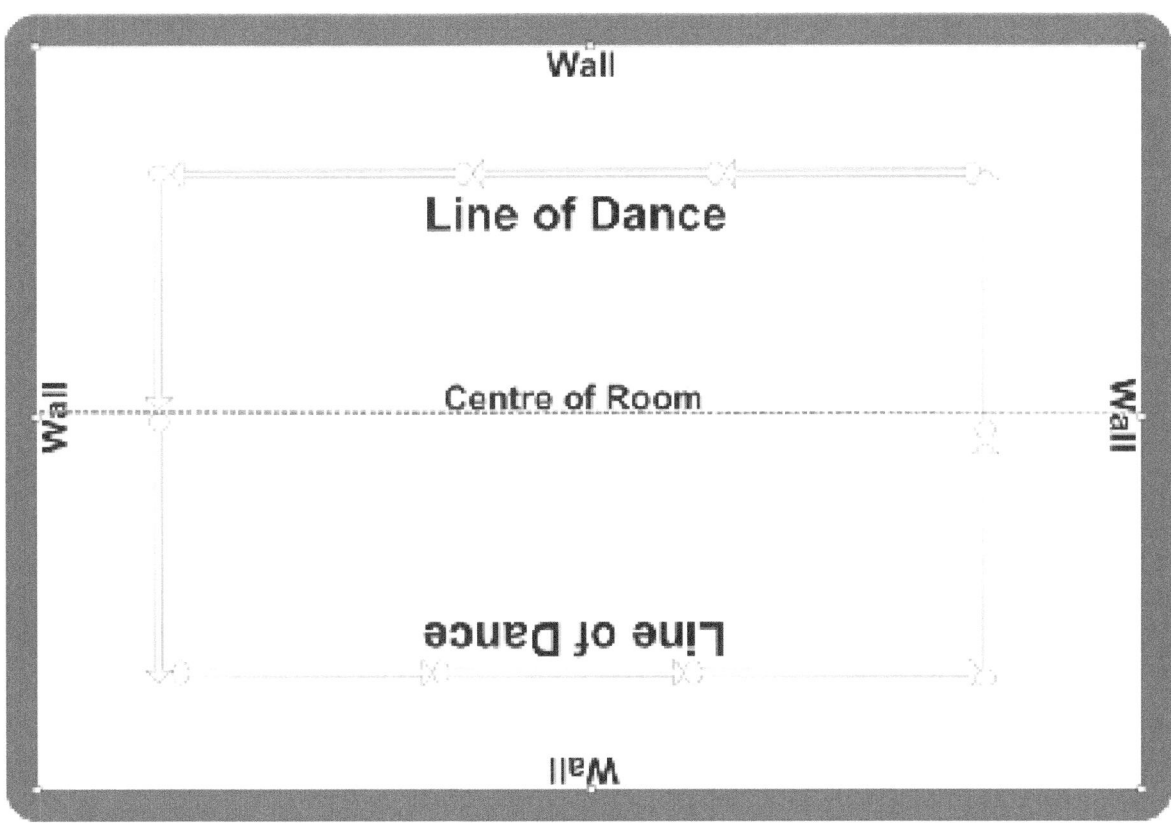

Reading the Charts

ALOD - Along Line of Dance
B - Backing
Back Ocho - A back walk with a pivot
Beat: Each number represents a quarter note of music equal to one quick count
Body Turns Less - When the body turns less than the foot direction
Cadencia - Rock Step
Caminada - Walking
CBMP - Contrary Body Movement Position (same track)
Chassé - Triple Step
Corrida - To Run
Count: The timing is given as a slow or a quick
DW - Diagonal to Wall
F - Facing
Fallaway Position - A Promenade Position that moves backward
Foot Position: Refers to the direction of the moving foot in relation to the other foot.
Forward Ocho - A forward walk with a pivot
FW - Facing Wall
L - Left
LF - Left Foot
LOD - Line of Dance
LSL - Left Side Leading (body)
Molinete - Windmill, Giro, Grapevine (describes the follower's step)
OP - Outside Partner
OPL - Leader steps outside on lady's left side
PP - Promenade Position, a V-shaped dance position with leader's left side and follower's right side slightly open.
R - Right
Rebote - Rebound
Reloj - Clock, turning side steps
RF - Right Foot
RSL - Right Side Leading (body)
Sacada - To displace and then take the place of
Salida - Exit, departure, or leave
Soltada - To Release
Turn: Amount of turn measured between the feet.

Tango Milonga Step List

01	**Walking with Traspié**
02	**Walking with Left Turn & Traspié**
03	**Forward Serpentine Combination**
04	**Forward & Back Traspié**
05	**Molinete Right with Sacada**
06	**Right Foot Cadencias Turning**
07	**Cadencia Cross Variation**
08	**Corrida**
09	**Rebound Both Sides (Corte)**
10	**Back Ochos**
11	**Turning Traspié & Chassé**
12	**Traspié Right Turn Combination**
13	**Ocho Cortado Continuous Cross**
14	**Ocho Cortado Forward & Back Variation**
15	**Soltada Leader's Solo Turn**

01 Walking with Traspié

Leader

Commence FLOD

Step#	Foot Position	Count	Turn (Feet)	Summary	Beat
1	LF Side, Part Weight	Q	Nil	Salida side with Traspié	1
2	RF Replace, Part Weight	Q	Nil		2
3	LF Side	S	Nil		3,4
4	RF Forward (CBMP) OP, Part Weight	Q	Nil	Caminada with Traspié	5
5	LF Replace, Part Weight	Q	Nil		6
6	RF Forward (CBMP) OP	S	Nil		7,8
7	LF Forward, Part Weight	Q	Nil	Resolution with Traspié	1
8	RF Replace, Part Weight	Q	Nil		2
9	LF Forward	S	Nil		3,4
10	RF Side, Part Weight	Q	Nil		5
11	LF Replace, Part Weight	Q	Nil		6
12	RF Side	S	Nil		7,8

Note: Keep your weight in the middle of both feet during the Traspié. Make your intention of movement clear, meaning indicate with your body the next direction of dance at the end of every Traspié. (step #3, #6 and #9)

Try dancing the first Traspié with slight rise and the second Traspié (OP) with a slight lowering.

01 Walking with Traspié

Follower

Commence BLOD

Step#	Foot Position	Count	Turn (Feet)	Summary	Beat
1	RF Side, Part Weight	Q	Nil	Salida side with Traspié	1
2	LF Replace, Part Weight	Q	Nil		2
3	RF Side	S	Nil		3,4
4	LF Back (CBMP) Part Weight	Q	Nil	Caminada with Traspié	5
5	RF Replace, Part Weight	Q	Nil		6
6	LF Back (CBMP)	S	Nil		7,8
7	RF Back, Part Weight	Q	Nil	Resolution with Traspié	1
8	LF Replace, Part Weight	Q	Nil		2
9	RF Back	S	Nil		3,4
10	LF Side, Part Weight	Q	Nil		5
11	RF Replace, Part Weight	Q	Nil		6
12	LF Side	S	Nil		7,8

Note: Pay close attention when changing you're dancing from Tango Lisa (stepping on every beat) to dancing part weight in the Traspié. It's even more important to stay in a close embrace to feel the leader's weight transfer when dancing the Traspié QQS.

02 Walking with Left Turn & Traspié

Leader

Commence FLOD

Step#	Foot Position	Count	Turn (Feet)	Summary	Beat
1	LF Side, Part Weight	Q	Nil	Salida side with Traspié	1
2	RF Replace, Part Weight	Q	Nil		2
3	LF Side	S	Nil		3,4
4	RF Forward (CBMP) OP, Part Weight	Q	Nil	Caminada with Traspié	5
5	LF Replace, Part Weight	Q	Nil		6
6	RF Forward (CBMP) OP	S	Nil		7,8
7	LF Forward	S	3/8 Turn to Left Over Steps 7 to 9	Walking with Left Turn	1,2
8	RF Side & Slightly Back	S			3,4
9	LF Back (CBMP) Part Weight	Q		Traspié	5
10	RF Replace, Part Weight	Q	Nil		6
11	LF Back (CBMP)	S	Nil		7,8
12	RF Back, Part Weight	Q	1/8 Turn to Left	Traspié	1
13	LF Replace, Part Weight	Q	Nil		2
14	RF Back	S	Nil		3,4
15	LF Side & Slightly Forward	S	3/8 Turn to Left	Salida to OP	5,6
16	RF Forward (CBMP) OP	S	Nil		7,8
17	LF Forward, Part Weight	Q	1/8 Turn to Left	Resolution with Traspié	1
18	RF Replace, Part Weight	Q	Nil		2
19	LF Forward	S	Nil		3,4
20	RF Side	S	Nil	Side Close	5,6
21	LF Closes to RF	S	Nil		7,8

Note: As it is only the feet that step outside partner, maintain your embrace and keep your partner in front of you.

02 Walking with Left Turn & Traspié

Follower

Commence BLOD

Step#	Foot Position	Count	Turn (Feet)	Summary	Beat
1	RF Side, Part Weight	Q	Nil	Salida side with Traspié	1
2	LF Replace, Part Weight	Q	Nil		2
3	RF Side	S	Nil		3,4
4	LF Back (CBMP) Part Weight	Q	Nil	Caminada with Traspié	5
5	RF Replace, Part Weight	Q	Nil		6
6	LF Back (CBMP)	S	Nil		7,8
7	RF Back	S	3/8 Turn to Left Over Steps 7 to 9	Walking with Left Turn	1,2
8	LF Side & Slightly Forward	S			3,4
9	RF Forward (CBMP) OP, Part Weight	Q		Traspié	5
10	LF Replace with Part Weight	Q	Nil		6
11	RF Forward (CBMP) OP	S	Nil		7,8
12	LF Forward, Part Weight	Q	1/8 Turn to Left	Traspié	1
13	RF Replace, Part Weight	Q	Nil		2
14	LF Forward	S	Nil		3,4
15	RF Side & Slightly Back	S	3/8 Turn to Left	Salida	5,6
16	LF Back (CBMP)	S	Nil		7,8
17	RF Back, Part Weight	Q	1/8 Turn to Left	Resolution with Traspié	1
18	LF Replace, Part Weight	Q	Nil		2
19	RF Back	S	Nil		3,4
20	LF Side	S	Nil	Side Close	5,6
21	RF Closes to LF	S	Nil		7,8

Note: Maintain your embrace and stay in front of the leader on step #9 when stepping outside partner.

03   Forward Serpentine Combination

Leader

Commence FLOD

Step#	Foot Position	Count	Turn (Feet)	Summary	Beat
1	LF Rock Forward	Q	Nil	Cadencia	1
2	RF Rock Back	Q	Nil		2
3	LF Side, Part Weight	Q	1/8 Turn to Right	Traspié	3
4	RF Replace Weight	Q			4
5	LF Forward (CBMP) OPL	S	Nil	Serpentine	5,6
6	RF Point with No Weight	S	1/4 Turn to Left (Body Turns Less)		7,8
7	RF Forward (CBMP) OP	S	Nil		1,2
8	LF Point with No Weight	S	1/4 Turn to Right (Body Turns Less)		3,4
9	LF Forward (CBMP) OPL	S	Nil		5,6
10	RF Point with No Weight	S	Nil (Body Turns to L)		7,8
11	RF Forward (CBMP) OP	S	1/8 Turn to Left (Body Turns Less)	Caminada	1,2
12	LF Forward	S	Nil	Resolution	3,4
13	RF Side	S	Nil		5,6
14	LF Closes to RF	S	Nil		7,8

Note: **Body turns less means keep your shoulders facing your partner while the feet step outside in CBMP.**

03   Forward Serpentine Combination

Follower

Commence BLOD

Step#	Foot Position	Count	Turn (Feet)	Summary	Beat
1	RF Rock Back	Q	Nil	Cadencia	1
2	LF Rock Forward	Q	Nil		2
3	RF Side, Part Weight	Q	1/8 Turn to Right	Traspié	3
4	LF Replace Weight	Q			4
5	RF Back (CBMP)	S	Nil	Serpentine	5,6
6	LF Point with No Weight	S	1/4 Turn to Left (Body Turns Less)		7,8
7	LF Back (CBMP)	S	Nil		1,2
8	RF Point with No Weight	S	1/4 Turn to Right (Body Turns Less)		3,4
9	RF Back (CBMP)	S	Nil		5,6
10	LF Point with No Weight	S	1/8 Turn to Left (Body Turns Less)		7,8
11	LF Back (CBMP)	S	Nil	Caminada	1,2
12	RF Back	S	Nil	Resolution	3,4
13	LF Side	S	Nil		5,6
14	RF Closes to LF	S	Nil		7,8

Note: On step #7 turn the body less than the pointing foot to allow the leader to step outside partner on step #8. The body turns less on every pointing step to keep the shoulders parallel to the leader.

04   Forward & Back Traspié

Leader

Commence FLOD

Step#	Foot Position	Count	Turn (Feet)	Summary	Beat
1	LF Side	S	1/8 Turn to Left (Body Turns Less)	Salida Side	1,2
2	RF Forward (CBMP) OP, Part Weight	Q	Nil	Traspié Forward	3
3	LF Replace Weight	Q	Nil		4
4	RF Side, Part Weight	Q	1/4 Turn to Right Over Steps 4 to 5 (Body Turns Less)	Traspié Side	5
5	LF Replace Weight	Q			6
6	RF Back, (CBMP) Part Weight	Q	Nil	Traspié Back	7
7	LF Replace Weight	Q	Nil		8
8	RF Side, Part Weight	Q	1/4 Turn to Left Over Steps 8 & 9 (Body Turns Less)	Traspié Side	1
9	LF Replace Weight	Q			2
10	RF Forward (CBMP) OP, Part Weight	Q	Nil	Traspié Forward	3
11	LF Replace Weight	Q	Nil		4
12	RF Side, Part Weight	Q	1/4 Turn to Right Over Steps 12 & 13 (Body Turns Less)	Traspié Side	5
13	LF Replace Weight	Q			6
14	RF Forward (CBMP) OP	S	Nil	Caminada	7,8

Note: 1. This pattern is very stationary. 2. Make all the Traspié steps very small. 3. Transfer as little weight as possible over the 12 "quicks". 4. Keep the LF stationary as you turn during the 12 quicks. This figure ends FDW.

04 Forward & Back Traspié
Follower

Commence BLOD

Step#	Foot Position	Count	Turn (Feet)	Summary	Beat
1	RF Side	S	1/8 Turn to Left (Body Turns Less)	Salida Side	1,2
2	LF Back (CBMP) Part Weight	Q	Nil	Traspié Back	3
3	RF Replace Weight	Q	Nil		4
4	LF Side, Part Weight	Q	1/4 Turn to Right (Body Turns Less)	Traspié Side	5
5	RF Replace Weight	Q			6
6	LF Forward (CBMP) OPL, Part Weight	Q	Nil	Traspié Forward	7
7	RF Replace Weight	Q	Nil		8
8	LF Side, Part Weight	Q	1/4 Turn to Left (Body Turns Less)	Traspié Side	1
9	RF Replace Weight	Q	Nil		2
10	LF Back (CBMP) Part Weight	Q	Nil	Traspié Back	3
11	RF Replace Weight	Q	Nil		4
12	LF Side, Part Weight	Q	1/4 Turn to Right (Body Turns Less)	Traspié Side	5
13	RF Replace Weight	Q			6
14	LF Back (CBMP)	S	Nil	Caminada	7,8

Note: Traspié steps back should be danced with forward body intention towards the leader. If you transfer too much weight backward, you will pull the leader.

05   Molinete Right with Sacada

Leader

Commence FLOD

Step#	Foot Position	Count	Turn (Feet)	Summary	Beat
1	LF Forward in Half Time	S S	Nil	Walks in Half Time	1,2 3,4
2	RF Forward in Half Time	S S	Nil		5,6 7,8
3	LF Forward	S	Nil	Caminada	1,2
4	RF Forward (CBMP) OP	S	Nil		3,4
5	LF Forward LSL	S	Nil		5,6
6	RF Crosses Behind LF (Lead Follower's Cross & Uncross)	S	Nil	Follower's Cross	7,8
7	LF Side (Small Step)	S	1/4 Turn to Right	Lead Molinete R Sacada with RF Exit with a Walk to OP	1,2
8	RF Forward Sacada (Between Follower's Feet)	S	3/8 Turn to Right		3,4
9	LF Forward LSL	S	3/8 Turn to Right		5,6
10	RF Forward (CBMP) OP	S	Nil		7,8

Note: Dancing at half time can slow down and relax your dancing. **It takes control and patience.** *Start moving the feet but keep the chest from moving forward in order to delay the follower from stepping too early.*

The Sacada, on step #8 is a forward step between the followers feet. Do not hit her trailing foot. (Follower's RF)

05 Molinete Right with Sacada

Follower

Commence BLOD

Step#	Foot Position	Count	Turn (Feet)	Summary	Beat
1	RF Back in Half Time	S S	Nil	Walks in Half Time	1,2 3,4
2	LF Back in Half Time	S S	Nil		5,6 7,8
3	RF Back	S	Nil	Caminada	1,2
4	LF Back (CBMP)	S	Nil		3,4
5	RF Back RSL	S	Nil		5,6
6	LF Crosses in Front of RF (Cruzada & Uncross)	S	Uncross 1/8 to Left	Follower's Cross & Uncross	7,8
7	RF Forward (CBMP) OP	S	1/8 Turn to Right	Molinete R (Forward, Side, Back)	1,2
8	LF Side (Receive Sacada)	S	3/8 Turn to Right		3,4
9	RF Back RSL	S	3/8 Turn to Right	Walk Out	5,6
10	LF Back (CBMP)	S	Nil		7,8

Note: If the follower's body weight is forward over the balls of the feet, it makes it possible to feel when the leader is moving or creating the half time. Wait for the leader to step.

06 Right Foot Cadencias Turning

Leader

Commence FLOD

Step#	Foot Position	Count	Turn (Feet)	Summary	Beat
1	RF Side (Small Step), Heels Stay Close Together)	S	3/8 Turn to Right Over Steps 1 to 4	Reloj The Clock to R	1,2
2	LF Coses to RF	S			3,4
3	RF Side (Small Step), Heels Stay Close Together)	S			5,6
4	LF Coses to RF	S			7,8
5	RF Back	S	Nil	Salida Back	1,2
6	LF Forward LSL	S	3/8 Turn to Left	Caminada	3,4
7	RF Rock Forward (CBMP) OP	S	7/8 Turn to Left Over Steps 7 to 13	Right Foot Cadencias Turning (3)	5,6
8	LF Rock Back (CBMP)	S			7,8
9	RF Rock Forward (CBMP) OP	S			1,2
10	LF Rock Back (CBMP)	S			3,4
11	RF Rock Forward (CBMP) OP	S			5,6
12	LF Rock Back (CBMP)	S			7,8
13	RF Forward (CBMP) OP	S	Facing DW		1,2
14	LF Forward	S	Nil	Resolution	3,4
15	RF Side	S	1/8 Turn to Left		5,6
16	LF Closes to RF	S	Nil		7,8

Note: You may want to keep the right leg very close to the follower's leg or gently touching the follower's right leg during the Right Turn Cadencia. Release the leg contact on step #13 to prepare for the Resolution ending.

06 Right Foot Cadencias Turning

Follower

Commence BLOD

Step#	Foot Position	Count	Turn (Feet)	Summary	Beat
1	LF Side	S	3/8 Turn to Right Over Steps 1 to 4	Reloj The Clock to R	1,2
2	RF Coses to LF	S			3,4
3	LF Side	S			5,6
4	RF Coses to LF	S			7,8
5	LF Forward	S	Nil	Salida Back	1,2
6	RF Back RSL	S	3/8 Turn to Left	Caminada	3,4
7	LF Rock Back (CBMP)	S	7/8 Turn to Left Over Steps 7 to 13	Leader's Right Foot Cadencias Turning (3)	5,6
8	RF Rock Forward (CBMP)	S			7,8
9	LF Rock Back (CBMP)	S			1,2
10	RF Rock Forward (CBMP)	S			3,4
11	LF Rock Back (CBMP)				5,6
12	RF Rock Forward (CBMP)				7,8
13	LF Back (CBMP)		Backing DW		1,2
14	RF Back	S	Nil	Resolution	3,4
15	LF Side	S	1/8 Turn to Left		5,6
16	RF Closes to LF	S	Nil		7,8

Note: The Right Turning Cadencias are very small and danced almost on the spot. Keep the body weight forward so you stay in the leader's embrace and avoid pulling the leader.

07   Cadencia Cross Variation

Leader

Commence FLOD from Position 3

Step#	Foot Position	Count	Turn (Feet)	Summary	Beat
1	RF Forward (CBMP) OP	S	Nil	Caminada	1,2
2	LF Rock Forward (CBMP)	Q	Nil	Cadencia Cross Variation	3
3	RF Rock Back (CBMP)	Q	Nil	Cross & Uncross	4
4	LF Crosses in Front of RF (Uncross)	S	Nil		5,6
5	RF Forward (CBMP) OP	S	Nil	Caminada	7,8
6	LF Rock Forward (CBMP)	Q	Nil	Cadencia Cross Variation	1
7	RF Rock Back (CBMP)	Q	Nil	Cross & Uncross	2
8	LF Crosses in Front of RF (Uncross)	S	Nil		3,4
9	RF Forward (CBMP) OP	S	Nil	Caminada	5,6
10	LF Forward LSL	S	Nil		7,8
11	RF Closes to LF	S	Nil	Follower's Cross	1,2
12	LF Forward	S	Nil	Resolution	3,4
13	RF Side	S	Nil		5,6
14	LF Closes to RF	S	Nil		7,8

Note: On steps #4 & #8, lead the follower to cross behind and remember to turn the follower to uncross their feet before stepping outside partner on the next step.

07 Cadencia Cross Variation
Follower

Commence BLOD from Position 3

Step#	Foot Position	Count	Turn (Feet)	Summary	Beat
1	LF Back (CBMP)	S	Nil	Caminada	1,2
2	RF Rock Back (CBMP)	Q	Nil	Cadencia Cross Variation Cross & Uncross	3
3	LF Rock Forward (CBMP)	Q	Nil		4
4	RF Crosses Behind LF (Uncross)	S	Nil		5,6
5	LF Back (CBMP)	S	Nil	Caminada	7,8
6	RF Rock Back (CBMP)	Q	Nil	Cadencia Cross Variation Cross & Uncross	1
7	LF Rock Forward (CBMP)	Q	Nil		2
8	RF Crosses Behind LF (Uncross)	S	Nil		3,4
9	LF Back (CBMP)	S	Nil	Caminada	5,6
10	RF Back RSL	S	Nil		7,8
11	LF Crosses in Front of RF (Cruzada)	S	Nil	Follower's Cross	1,2
12	RF Back	S	Nil	Resolution	3,4
13	LF Side	S	Nil		5,6
14	RF Closes to LF	S	Nil		7,8

Note: On steps #4 & #8, keep the shoulders turned towards your partner in CBMP, this will encourage the cross behind. The uncross happens quickly, so accept the rotation lead. Preventing this rotation will make uncrossing impossible.

08 Corrida

Leader

Commence FLOD

Step#	Foot Position	Count	Turn (Feet)	Summary	Beat
1	LF Forward	Q	Nil	Corrida in Front of Follower	1
2	RF Forward	Q	Nil		2
3	LF Forward LSL	S	Nil		3,4
4	RF Forward (CBMP) OP	Q	Nil	From Position 3, Corrida to PP Leading Follower Back, Side Forward, Ending in PP	5
5	LF Forward	Q	Nil		6
6	RF Forward (CBMP) In PP	S	1/8 Turn to Right		7,8
7	LF Closes to RF with No Weight	S	1/8 Turn to Right	Rebote Forward	1,2
8	LF Back (CBMP) Fallaway Position	S	1/8 Turn to LLeft	Turn the Follower Back (Slow Back Ocho)	3,4
9	RF Closes to LF with No Weight	S	Nil		5,6
10	RF Forward (CBMP) OP	S	1/8 Turn to Left (Body Turns Less)	Caminada Position 3	7,8

Note: After the follower steps back on step# 4, lead the rotation. You must understand the follower's steps: (Back, Side, Forward) to lead it well. Focus on the follower's steps.

On step #7 stop the forward movement with a rebound action, bringing your partner from PP to closed position.

08   Corrida

Follower

Commence BLOD

Step#	Foot Position	Count	Turn (Feet)	Summary	Beat
1	RF Back	Q	Nil	Corrida	1
2	LF Back	Q	Nil		2
3	RF Back RSL	S	Nil		3,4
4	LF Back (CBMP)	Q	3/8 Turn to Right Over Steps 4 to 6	From Position 3, Corrida to PP Back, Side, Forward in PP	5
5	RF Side	Q			6
6	LF Forward (CBMP) In PP	S			7,8
7	RF Closes to LF with No Weight	S	1/8 Left	Rebote Forward	1,2
8	RF Back (CBMP) Fallaway Position	S	1/8 Right Then step to pivot 3/8 Left	Slow Back Ocho	3,4
9	LF Closes to RF with No Weight	S	1/4 Left		5,6
10	LF Back (CBMP)	S	1/8 Turn to Left (Body Turns Less)	Caminada Position 3	7,8

Note: All Corrida steps are quick and small. Pay attention to not move away from the leader or too far backward (on steps #1,2,3). Keep a relaxed embrace when turning over steps #4, #5 and #6. Adjust your hold in the embrace to make this comfortable for you.

09 Rebound Both Sides (Corte)

Leader

Commence FLOD

Step#	Foot Position	Count	Turn (Feet)	Summary	Beat
1	LF Side	S	Nil	Salida Side	1,2
2	RF Forward (CBMP) OP	S	Nil	Lead Molinete Follower Back, Side Forward	3,4
3	LF Position Held with No Weight	S	Nil (Body Turns L)		5,6
4	LF Closes to RF with No Weight	S	Nil (Body Turns L)		7,8
5	LF Position Held with No Weight	S	Nil (Body Turns L)	Rebound	1,2
6	LF Forward (CBMP) OPL	S	Nil	Lead Molinete Follower Back, Side Forward	3,4
7	RF Position Held with No Weight	S	Nil (Body Turns R)		5,6
8	RF Closes to RF with No Weight	S	Nil (Body Turns R)		7,8
9	RF Position Held with No Weight	S	Nil (Body Turns R)	Rebound	1,2
10	RF Forward (CBMP) OP	S	Nil	Lead Molinete Follower Back, Side Forward	3,4
11	LF Position Held with No Weight	S	Nil (Body Turns L)		5,6
12	LF Closes to RF with No Weight	S	Nil (Body Turns L)		7,8
13	LF Position Held with No Weight	S	Nil (Body Turns L)	Rebound	1,2
14	LF Forward (CBMP) OPL	S	Nil	Lead Follower Forward, Side, Close	3,4
15	RF Side (Small Step)	S	Nil (Body Turns R)		5,6
16	LF Closes to RF	S	Nil		7,8

Note: Create a smooth and constant body turn to lead the follower around on both sides. Use the rebound energy to restart the new direction of movement towards the opposite side.

Although the leader's feet don't turn, all the follower's rotation is created by the leader turning the shoulders from left to right.

09   Rebound Both Sides (Corte)
Follower

Commence BLOD

Step#	Foot Position	Count	Turn (Feet)	Summary	Beat
1	RF Side	S	Nil	Salida Side	1,2
2	LF Back (CBMP)	S	Nil	Molinete (Back, Side Forward)	3,4
3	RF Side	S	Nil		5,6
4	LF Forward (CBMP) OPL	S	1/8 Turn to Left		7,8
5	RF Closes to LF with No Weight	S	1/8 Turn to Left then 1/8 to Right	Rebound	1,2
6	RF Back (CBMP)	S	1/8 Turn to Right	Molinete (Back, Side Forward)	3,4
7	LF Side	S	Nil		5,6
8	RF Forward (CBMP) OP	S	1/8 Turn to Right		7,8
9	LF Closes to RF with No Weight	S	1/8 Turn to Right then 1/8 to Left	Rebound	1,2
10	LF Back (CBMP)	S	1/8 Turn to Left	Molinete (Back, Side Forward)	3,4
11	RF Side	S	Nil		5,6
12	LF Forward (CBMP) OPL	S	1/8 Turn to Left		7,8
13	RF Closes to LF with No Weight	S	1/8 Turn to Left then 1/8 to Right	Rebound	1,2
14	RF Back (CBMP)	S	1/8 Turn to Right	Back, Side, Close	3,4
15	LF Side	S	Nil		5,6
16	RF Closes to LF	S	Nil		7,8

Note: Just follow the leader's shoulders for the Molinete rotation and the amount of turn. Keep a relaxed and easy flow in the rebound.

10 Back Ochos

Leader

Commence FLOD

Step#	Foot Position	Count	Turn (Feet)	Summary	Beat
1	LF Rock Forward	Q	Nil	Cadencia	1
2	RF Rock Back	Q	Nil		2
3	LF Side	S	1/8 Turn to Left		3,4
4	RF Forward (CBMP) OP	S	Nil	Lead Back Ochos	5,6
5	LF Back (CBMP)	S	1/4 Turn to Left		7,8
6	RF Forward (CBMP) OP	S	1/4 Turn to Right		1,2
7	LF Back (CBMP)	S	1/4 Turn to Left		3,4
8	RF Forward (CBMP) OP	S	1/4 Turn to Right		5,6
9	LF Back (CBMP)	S	1/4 Turn to Left		7,8
10	RF Forward (CBMP) OP	S	1/4 Turn to Right	Caminada	1,2
11	LF Diagonally Forward	S	1/8 Turn to Right		3,4
12	RF Forward (CBMP) OP	S	Nil	To Position 3	5,6
13	LF Forward	S	Nil	Resolution	7,8
14	RF Side	S	Nil		1,2
15	LF Closes to RF	S	Nil		3,4
16	RF Side (Small Step), Heels Stay Close Together)	S	1/8 Right	Reloj The Clock to R	5,6
17	LF Closes to RF	S	Nil		7,8

Note: The amount of turn is given between the feet, but the shoulders stay facing the follower during steps #4 to #11. The leader will feel like there is no turn, and should instead think about turning the follower.
On step #9 turn the follower less (only 1/8) to adjust the end alignment walking out towards the LOD.

10 Back Ochos

Follower

Commence BLOD

Step#	Foot Position	Count	Turn (Feet)	Summary	Beat
1	RF Rock Back	Q	Nil	Cadencia	1
2	LF Rock Forward	Q	Nil		2
3	RF Side	S	1/8 Turn to Left		3,4
4	LF Back (same track) Pivot on LF	S	Step Then Pivot Right 1/4 on LF	Back Ochos	5,6
5	RF Back (same track) Pivot on RF	S	Step Then Pivot Left 1/4 on RF		7,8
6	LF Back (same track) Pivot on LF	S	Step Then Pivot Right 1/4 on LF		1,2
7	RF Back (same track) Pivot on RF	S	Step Then Pivot Left 1/4 on RF		3,4
8	LF Back (same track) Pivot on LF	S	Step Then Pivot Right 1/4 on LF		5,6
9	RF Back (same track) Pivot on RF	S	Step Then Pivot Left 1/8 on RF		7,8
10	LF Back (same track) Pivot on LF	S	Nil	Caminada	1,2
11	RF Back RSL	S	Nil		3,4
12	LF Back (CBMP)	S	Nil		5,6
13	RF Back	S	Nil	Resolution	7,8
14	LF Side	S	Nil		1,2
15	RF Closes to LF	S	Nil		3,4
16	LF Side	S	1/8 Right	Reloj The Clock to R	5,6
17	RF Closes to LF	S	Nil		7,8

Note: Due to the faster speed of Milonga, the Ochos are smaller in rotation. Allow the leader to initiate the movement on all your back walks. Wait for the leader's movement before stepping back. Notice the smaller pivot on step #9.

11 Turning Traspié & Chassé

Leader

Commence FLOD from Position 3

Step#	Foot Position	Count	Turn (Feet)	Summary	Beat
1	RF Forward (CBMP) OP, Part Weight	Q	3/8 Turn to Left Over steps 1 to 3	Traspié Turning Left	1
2	LF Replace, Part Weight	Q			2
3	RF Forward (CBMP) OP	S			3,4
4	LF Side	Q	1/8 Turn to Left Over steps 4 to 6	Chassé Turning Left	5
5	RF Closes to LF	Q			6
6	LF Side	S			7,8
7	RF Forward (CBMP) OP, Part Weight	Q	3/8 Turn to Left Over steps 7 to 9	Traspié Turning Left	1
8	LF Replace, Part Weight	Q			2
9	RF Forward (CBMP) OP	S			3,4
10	LF Side	Q	1/8 Turn to Left Over steps 10 to 12	Chassé Turning Left	5
11	RF Closes to LF	Q			6
12	LF Side	S			7,8

Note: Try dancing the Traspié with a slight lowering and the Chassé with a slight rise. Keep the Chassé step very small so the follower can stay in front of you. The embrace can be relaxed to allow a comfortable outside partner position during the Traspié Turning Left.

The Chassé Turning Left can be danced moving Diag Forward to make it easier for the follower to change from an outside partner position to back in front of the leader.

11 Turning Traspié & Chassé

Follower

Commence BLOD from Position 3

Step#	Foot Position	Count	Turn (Feet)	Summary	Beat
1	LF Back (CBMP), Part Weight	Q	3/8 Turn to Left Over steps 1 to 3	Traspié Turning Left	1
2	RF Replace, Part Weight	Q			2
3	LF Back (CBMP)	S			3,4
4	RF Side	Q	1/8 Turn to Left Over steps 4 to 6	Chassé Turning Left	5
5	LF Closes to RF	Q			6
6	RF Side	S			7,8
7	LF Back (CBMP), Part Weight	Q	3/8 Turn to Left Over steps 7 to 9	Traspié Turning Left	1
8	RF Replace, Part Weight	Q			2
9	LF Back (CBMP)	S			3,4
10	RF Side	Q	1/8 Turn to Left Over steps 10 to 12	Chassé Turning Left	5
11	LF Closes to RF	Q			6
12	RF Side	S			7,8

Note: The Traspié step is not a travelling step. Keep it almost in place while turning.

The Chassé Turning Left can be danced moving Diag Forward to make it easier for the follower to change from an outside partner position to back in front of the leader. Step #4 transitions from outside partner position back in front of the leader. Pay attention not to step into the leader's foot on this step #4.

12 Traspié Right Turn Combination

Leader

Commence FDC from Position 3

Step#	Foot Position	Count	Turn (Feet)	Summary	Beat
1	RF Forward (CBMP) OP, Part Weight	Q	Nil	Traspié Forward	1
2	LF Replace Weight	Q	Nil		2
3	RF Side, Part Weight	Q	1/4 Turn to Right Over Steps 3 to 4	Traspié Side	3
4	LF Replace Weight	Q			4
5	RF Back (CBMP) Part Weight	Q	Nil	Traspié Back	5
6	LF Replace Weight	Q	Nil		6
7	RF Forward	Q	1/8 Turn to Right	Right Turn	7
8	LF Side & Slightly Back	Q	1/8 Turn to Right		8
9	RF Back RSL	S	1/8 Right		1,2
10	LF Back (CBMP) (Small Step)	S	3/8 Turn to Right Over Steps 10 to 12 End Facing DC		3,4
11	RF Side (Small Step)	S			5,6
12	LF Forward LSL	S			7,8

Note: This step starts Facing Diagonal Center and ends Facing Diagonal Center. On steps #3 and #4 relax the embrace and rotate the follower to step outside partner to the leader's left side. Make sure step #8 is wide to allow the follower to continue OP for the Right Turn. Prepare a right side lead on step #9 to allow the follower to step outside partner on step #10.

12   Traspié Right Turn Combination

Follower

Commence BDC from Position 3

Step#	Foot Position	Count	Turn (Feet)	Summary	Beat
1	LF Back (CBMP) Part Weight	Q	Nil	Traspié Back	1
2	RF Replace Weight	Q	Nil		2
3	LF Side, Part Weight	Q	1/8 Turn to Right	Traspié Side	3
4	RF Replace Weight	Q	1/8 Turn to Right		4
5	LF Forward (CBMP) OP, Part Weight	Q	Nil	Traspié Forward	5
6	RF Replace Weight	Q	Nil		6
7	LF Back	Q	1/8 Turn to Right	Right Turn	7
8	RF Side & Slightly Forward	Q	1/8 Turn to Right		8
9	LF Forward RSL	S	1/8 Turn to Right		1,2
10	RF Forward (CBMP)	S	1/8 Turn to Right		3,4
11	LF Side	S	3/8 Turn to Right		5,6
12	RF Back RSL	S	Nil		7,8

Note: Try looking to your right side at the leader's left shoulder on steps #3 and #4 to make the OP dance position easier. Stay in front of your partner on step #10, only taking a step as wide as the rotation of the leader's shoulder.

13   Ocho Cortado Continuous Cross

Leader

Commence FDW

Step#	Foot Position	Count	Turn (Feet)	Summary	Beat
1	LF Side	S	1/8 Turn to Left (Body Turns Less)	Salida Side	1,2
2	RF Forward (CBMP) OP	S	Nil	Caminada	3,4
3	LF Rock Forward	Q	Nil	Cadencia	5
4	RF Rock Back	Q	Nil		6
5	LF Back (CBMP)	S	Nil		7,8
6	RF Side (Small Step) Part Weight	Q	1/8 Right	Ocho Cortado	1
7	LF Replace Weight	Q	1/8 Left Over Steps 7 to 8		2
8	RF Closes to LF (Slightly Back) Lead Follower's Cross	S		Follower's Cross	3,4
9	LF Side (small step) (heels stay close together on side steps for the Clock)	Q	Clock (reloj) Gradually Continue Turning Left for One Complete Turn	Continuous Crosses for Follower	5
10	RF Closes to LF	Q		Lead Followers's Cross on steps 10, 12, 14, 16, 18, 20	6
11	LF Side (small step)	Q			7
12	RF Closes to LF	Q			8
13	LF Side (small step)	Q			1
14	RF Closes to LF	Q			2
15	LF Side (small step)	Q			3
16	RF Closes to LF	Q			4
17	LF Side (small step)	Q			5
18	RF Closes to LF	Q			6
19	LF Side (small step)	Q			7
20	RF Closes to LF	Q			8

Note: Keep the follower in a close embrace and encourage an inner movement to create the follower's continuous cross steps. Your left hand should not move outward; keep a normal embrace. There is no PP position.

13 Ocho Cortado Continuous Cross

Follower

Commence BDW

Step#	Foot Position	Count	Turn (Feet)	Summary	Beat
1	RF Side	S	1/8 Turn to Left (Body Turns Less)	Salida Side	1,2
2	LF Back (CBMP)	S	Nil	Caminada	3,4
3	RF Rock Back	Q	Nil	Cadencia	5
4	LF Rock Forward	Q	Nil		6
5	RF Forward (CBMP) OP	S	Nil		7,8
6	LF Side, Part Weight	Q	1/8 Right	Ocho Cortado	1
7	RF Replace Weight	Q	1/8 Left Over Steps 7 to 8		2
8	LF Cross in Front of RF	S		Follower's Cross	3,4
9	RF Side	Q	Gradually Continue Turning Left for One Complete Turn	Continuous Crosses for Follower	5
10	LF Crosses in Front of RF	Q			6
11	RF Side	Q			7
12	LF Crosses in Front of RF	Q			8
13	RF Side	Q			1
14	LF Crosses in Front of RF	Q			2
15	RF Side	Q			3
16	LF Crosses in Front of RF	Q			4
17	RF Side	Q			5
18	LF Crosses in Front of RF	Q			6
19	RF Side	Q			7
20	LF Crosses in Front of RF	Q			8

Note: Feel the intention of movement that moves you slightly forward to cross. Cross directly in front of the leader.

14 Ocho Cortado Forward & Back Variation

Leader

Commence FDW

Step#	Foot Position	Count	Turn (Feet)	Summary	Beat
1	LF Side	S	1/8 Turn to Left (Body Turns Less)	Salida Side	1,2
2	RF Forward (CBMP) OP	S	Nil	Caminada	3,4
3	LF Rock Forward	Q	Nil	Cadencia	5
4	RF Rock Back	Q	Nil		6
5	LF Back (CBMP)	S	Nil		7,8
6	RF Side (Small Step) Part Weight	Q	1/8 Turn to Right	Ocho Cortado to PP and then Traspié in PP	1
7	LF Replace Weight	Q	Nil		2
8	RF Forward (CBMP) PP, Part Weight	Q	Nil		3
9	LF Replace Weight	Q	Nil		4
10	RF Side (Slightly Back) Part Weight	Q	Nil	Traspié turning Follower to Step Back in Position 3	5
11	LF Replace Weight	Q	Nil		6
12	RF Forward (CBMP) OP	S	Nil		7,8

Note: Pay attention to the amount of turn for the follower and make this clear in your lead. Do not over extend your left arm for the PP position.

14 Ocho Cortado Forward & Back Variation

Follower

Commence BDW

Step#	Foot Position	Count	Turn (Feet)	Summary	Beat
1	RF Side	S	1/8 Turn to Left (Body Turns Less)	Salida Side	1,2
2	LF Back (CBMP)	S	Nil	Caminada	3,4
3	RF Rock Back	Q	Nil	Cadencia	5
4	LF Rock Forward	Q	Nil		6
5	RF Forward (CBMP) OP	S	Nil		7,8
6	LF Side, Part Weight	Q	3/8 Turn to Right	Ocho Cortado to PP and then Traspié to PP	1
7	RF Replace Weight	Q			2
8	LF Forward (CBMP) PP, Part Weight	Q	Nil		3
9	RF Replace Weight	Q	Nil		4
10	LF Side, Part Weight	Q	1/4 Turn to Left Over Steps 10 to 11	Traspié Turning Back to Position 3	5
11	RF Replace Weight	Q			6
12	LF Back (CBMP)	S	1/8 Turn to Left (Body Turns Less)		7,8

Note: Be very light on your feet during the Ocho Cortado and Traspié. You need to react and rotate quickly.

15   Soltada Leader's Solo Turn

Leader

Commence FLOD

Step#	Foot Position	Count	Turn (Feet)	Summary	Beat
1	LF Side	S	1/8 Turn to Left	Salida Side	1,2
2	RF Back (CBMP) Cross Behind	S	1/4 Turn to Right	Lead Back Ocho	3,4
3	LF Forward (Release Hold) Solo Turn	S	Nil (Body Turns Right)	Lead Molinete Follower Back, Side, Forward	5,6
4	RF Forward	S	1/8 Turn to Left		7,8
5	LF Side (Take Embrace)	S	3/8 Turn to Left		1,2
6	RF Closes to LF	S	1/4 Turn to Right	Caminada	3,4
7	LF Forward	S	1/8 Turn to Right		5,6
8	RF Closes to LF	S	Nil	Close	7,8

Note: On step #3, even though you release the embrace, remembember to use your shoulder rotation to indicate the Molinete action for the follower. On step #5 start to regain the embrace. On step #6 close your feet while slowing down the rotation and inviting the follower to end in front of you returning to a close embrace.

15 Soltada Leader's Solo Turn

Follower

Commence BLOD

Step#	Foot Position	Count	Turn (Feet)	Summary	Beat
1	RF Side	S	1/8 Turn to Left	Salida Side	1,2
2	LF Back (same track) Pivot on LF	S	Step Then Pivot 1/4 Right	Back Ocho	3,4
3	RF Back (CBMP) (Release Hold)	S	1/8 (Body Turns Right)	Molinete Back, Side, Forward	5,6
4	LF Side	S	1/4 Turn to Right		7,8
5	RF Forward (CBMP) (Take Embrace)	S	1/8 Turn to Right		1,2
6	LF Side	S	1/4 Turn to Right	Caminada	3,4
7	RF Back	S	1/8 Turn to Right		5,6
8	LF Closes to RF	S	Nil	Close	7,8

Note: When the leader releases hold during the Back Ocho, continue with a normal Molinete (Back, Side, Forward) until the leader regains hold.

Canadian Dance Federation (CDF) Student Medal Program

What is the Student Medal Program?
This is a great way for the student to learn to dance through a structured set of exams. It gives the student concrete goals and certification of their progress. A student exam motivates them. Students learn a wide variety of dance figures from the syllabus, dance them to a routine and eventually improvise at a more advanced level. Each student receives a certification after passing each level of exam.
A National Examiner conducts the exam.

Professional Argentine Tango CDF Exams
Become a better teacher. Expand your understanding of dance concepts, improve your presentation skills, teach precise vocabulary, sharpen your knowledge.

You are required to know and dance both the leader and follower's role. Achieve a standard of professional excellence.

CDF offers four levels of Argentine Tango professional certification:
Bronze, Silver, Gold and Platinum.

Contact:
https://www.canadiandancesportfederation.ca/
Phone: (888) 882-7285
Email: info@canadiandancesportfederation.ca